A Day at the Museum

by Sibel Sagner, Sevi Senocak
and Inci Kartal
illustrated by Moni Perez

CAMBRIDGE
UNIVERSITY PRESS

UCL
Institute of Education

Omar and his friends were excited.
They were going to a museum.

Miss Garcia put the children in groups.

'You can go and look,' she said, 'but you must not touch. Some of the things are very old.'

Omar, Beno and Zara saw some dolls.

'Look at this little man doll,'
said Zara. 'He is very old.'

'He looks older than my grandpa,'
said Beno.

Zara and Omar laughed.

Miss Garcia asked the children to pick something to draw.

'I'm going to draw the little man doll,' said Zara. 'He's sweet.'

'I want to look at the horse bones,' said Omar.

'Did you know that horses have 205 bones?' said Omar.

'Wow!' said Zara.

'I'm going to draw the horse bones,' said Omar.

Beno saw a yo-yo.

'Look at this old yo-yo,' he said.
'I can make it go up and down.'

Beno played with the yo-yo.

'Put it down, Beno,' said Zara.
'Miss Garcia said not to touch
the toys. She will be cross.'

The yo-yo went up in the air.

'Oh, no!' shouted Omar.

Zara grabbed the yo-yo.

'I said please do not touch
the toys,' said Miss Garcia.

Omar showed his picture
to Miss Garcia.

'I had a good time,' he said.

'Can we make a museum at school?' asked Zara.

'What a wonderful idea,' said Miss Garcia.

The next day Miss Garcia brought some big bags to school.

Miss Garcia said, 'We are going to make a museum.'

'Oh, no!' said Omar.
'What can I use for the 205 bones?'

A Day at the Museum ✦ S Sagner, S Senocak and I Kartal

Teaching notes written by Sue Bodman and Glen Franklin

Using this book

Developing reading comprehension

This is a book in the International School strand of the Cambridge Reading Adventure series featuring Omar and his friends. In this story, the children visit a museum, and Zara has a good idea. But Omar has a problem to solve at the end. The story has a sequence of events, occuring over time and in different venues. Pictures support the storyline rather than illustrating the exact meaning, requiring more inferential reading.

Grammar and sentence structure

- Sentence patterns and structures are more varied.
- Speech is sustained over more than one sentence.

Word meaning and spelling

- Fast automatic recognition of high-frequency words.
- Decoding new and unfamiliar words, supported by context and meaning.

Curriculum links

Science – Study of animal bones and skeletons. Linked to work on fossils and dinosaur bones.

History – Beno says the doll looks older than his grandpa. Children could ask grandparents about toys they played with when they were young. How were they different to modern-day toys?

Learning Outcomes

Children can:

- solve unfamiliar words using print information and understanding of the text
- sustain accurate reading over a greater number of lines of text on a page

- comment on events, characters, and ideas, making imaginative links to their own experience.

A guided reading lesson

Book Introduction

Give each child a copy of the book. Read the title and the blurb with them. Remind the children that they have read other books about Omar and his friends. Children might read some of the earlier International School stories prior to this guided reading lesson.

Orientation

Ask the children if they have ever been to a museum (perhaps as part of a school trip). Talk about the different things found in a museum.

Remind the children of (or establish) the characters in the story. Give a brief overview of the book:

In this book, Omar and his friends visit a museum with their teacher, Miss Garcia. They were very excited. I wonder what they will see there.

Preparation

Page 3: *Miss Garcia told the children they must not touch anything in the museum. Why not? Yes, it says here, 'They are very old'. Do you think anyone will touch? Who might that be?*

Page 4: Draw attention to the picture of the children laughing. Say: *Look at the text and see if it tells you why. Do you think the doll was really older than Beno's grandpa?* Point out the two syllables in 'grand/pa', particularly attending to the last syllable /pa/. Some children may be tempted to substitute their own family name here, such as 'grandad' or 'grandfather'.

Pages 6 and 7: Ensure the children understand that Omar has chosen to draw